Brain Rot

Meghan Richardson

BookLeaf
Publishing

Presentation by *BookLeaf Publishing*

Web: www.bookleafpub.com

E-mail: info@bookleafpub.com

ISBN: 9789357744232

First edition 2023

To Nath, Armee, Darby. I wouldn't have made it this far without you.

To mum and grandma, I wish you were here to read it.

ACKNOWLEDGEMENT

I'd like to thank my extension English teacher in year 12 who told me I was not very good at creative writing.

PREFACE

Brain Rot is a collection of poems I've been writing since I was 15, so the quality varies. Nonetheless, every poem represents a different point in my life.

Nostalgia For Something I Hated

I can never go home.
My old bedroom is sitting in a storage locker
packed up in boxes and
covered in mould.
We'll go back for it someday.

I didn't mind when the old Blockbuster closed.
Or when they paved over the park.
I didn't cry when everyone moved away.
Or when the house was sold.

Oh, but you hate going home.
It's so boring. So mundane.
The yapping dog and the sizzling telephone
poles.
Mum is telling you a long story about the
grocery store
Dad is...
well, he's there.
and the neighbourhood never changes.
The stale scent is a perfume of its own.
No one ever moves away.
Oh god, what strange hell for you
To be home.

There's history wrapped up in newspaper.
Tucked away to preserve it.
Time eats away at you like mould.
You're just a slab of meat at its whim.
Say you never liked it there anyway.

What was left of your good intentions has
started to spoil.
Cardboard boxes and packing peanuts
 never made to last this long.

I was abandoned like luggage
Whose contents are better forgotten.
One day it will be taken
Languishingly plucked out of you.
Like they were still trying to preserve it.
A rotten carcass wrapped up in newspaper.

I'd like to go home.
I cut off my stems and lay in freshwater.
I try not to go bad and go bitter.
"What do you want me to say?"
All the boxes and the memories are covered in:
Flies and vomit and shit and mould.
My good intentions
Have completely rotted away.

I remember everything.
But you don't.
You remember the tang of cough medicine.
The crispy bite of a bag of wine.
I could drive around the old streets
but the telegraph poles don't sizzle the way they
used to.
The Blockbuster is an apartment block.
My friends all moved away.
I wish I could go home to before.

Why is it all decaying?
Every time you remember it
you wear down a little more.
But it's nice,
To remember,
Anyway.

I was just a child.
Time marches on,
'Til you're stuffed with maggots and gagging.
Until it eats you from the inside out.
You can't ignore me anymore.

I want to go home.
A white picket fence with
a yapping dog.
Maybe it's not real.

But it's nice,
to remember,
anyway.

My Inheritance

Don't acknowledge it!
It sits buzzing and oozing in the corner.
I came by it honestly.
I inherited my mother's, too.
I can't throw them out-
They're non-biodegradable.

You must learn to live with it.
If you throw a rug over it it could be:
a strangely shaped lounge or a personality quirk.
Don't stare for too long.

I try to make friends
But I fear they can smell it when I open my
mouth.
I squeeze my lips together and tuck it away in
my cheeks.
It's actually a smile.

Sometimes there are flowers.
Sometimes without warning,
they rip out all the flowers
and spread manure in the garden
so the whole park smells like shit.

It takes a wicked sense of humour
ruin the best years of your life
But if love was a song or a beautiful melody
I was a dying pig squealing the tune.

Dear Mum

There are parts of you that linger
Long after you're gone
Your clothes still smell like you
Even after you died, I notice you all the time

I hear your favourite song on the radio.
I have your fingers and nose.
I whisper your name to the stars.
I still notice you everywhere.

I tried to bury you
Deep inside the void of my chest
but during the night you claw your way out
and I must stitch the wounds each morning

She taught me everything I know:
how to make instant coffee
to say hello and salutations
and the best spots to hide empty vodka bottles.

I know about her demons
She presented them to me
Wrapped in pink tissue paper
and an umbilical cord

I know why you are the way that you were
You were just a child
You deserved more
Then broken beer bottles
and wandering hands

But mama, I was just a kid
Did I really deserve
To go through the same?
What didn't kill us
Never made us stronger anyway.

God, I miss you.
Every single day.
I miss you like a child.
But sometimes I thank god
that you can't hurt me anymore.

Race You to Hell But I'll Let You Win

I crawled quickly out of the water.
Wasn't sure if I'd be followed.
All that mud that you've been slinging -
I've done much worse than you thought of.

I'm a sinner, you're a saint.
I know a sucker when I see one.
How much does your conscience weigh?
Are you dying to be forgiven?

If you want me, come and get me.
I'm just waiting round the corner.
Do you believe in heaven's gates?
I'm not anybody's daughter.

Did you want hell?
Did you want angels?
Have you catholic motivations?
Did you want me on my knees?
Good sir, what are your intentions?

The End

I heard the sun is going to explode tomorrow.
I heard the government putting funky kool-aid in
all the drinking water.
I heard there's gonna be a silent black hole that
swallows everything.
I heard there's a plague and a nuclear bomb
and no one is going to make it out alive.

I can't wait for tomorrow.
Let the world end.
I'm so tired.

Human flesh is weak.
My skin is paper-thin.
These human bodies of ours
are fragile
so fragile
One nasty germ
Smaller than the smallest thing you can see
to wipe us all out.

My Love

I will place my feverish lips
over the soft skin of your
arctic hips,
and kiss hard enough to
leave a bruise
the size of a peach,
and whisper
did you miss me?

I blink it in Morse code
carve it into your femur bones
send smoke signals
and carrier pigeons
but I cannot say it out loud
I still wonder
do you feel the same?

I cannot be close enough
I entwine our fingers
press my body against yours
shove my tongue inside your mouth
but it's still not close enough
atoms are 99% empty space
I wish I knew what you were thinking

Oh F***

I'm losing the plot.
With sweaty palms and aching fingertips.
My knuckles flushed white and strained to hold
it.
My grip is unstable.
My fingers are slippery.
My mind is unsteady.
Sections of the plot drip around my fingertips.
Like I've dipped my hands in salt
and started squeezing ice cubes.
I thought I was holding on tightly.
But I already lost it.

Oh fuck,
such deafening silence.
With my fingers clinging.
My throat has closed.
Sealed shut around the words.
Everything I should say sits stale
and rotting.
Squashed underneath a heavy tongue.
There's not a syllable I want to say
that I'm willing to let you hear

Perfection

You only drink decaf.
One glass of wine every two weeks.
Wake up at 5 am.
To go on long walks in your neighbourhood.
You are watching the forest burn down.

You take photos of the sunrise.
Never kill spiders.
Pick them up in a glass cup and
set them free on perfectly cut grass.
You can hear the sirens getting closer.

You take your medication.
With lemon water and ice cubes.
Smiling at strangers on the street.
Thanking the bus driver.
You cannot run away from the flames.

They find your body.
Almost burnt to a crisp.
In the middle of the ash
with a matchbox clutched tightly in your fist
They will not think of you
as healthy and well-adjusted

Home

You feel like home.
I have been a tiny rowboat,
untethered all my life.
I have been an abandoned luggage,
waiting in an airport.
I have been a rock,
drowning in a peat bog.

You feel like home.
You are my home.

Please come home to me.

Letter To My Friends

15

This is a letter,
To let you know that I'm still thinking of you.
That I'll always remember you
and be proud of you.

This is a letter to say
That I still love you
I wish you nothing but happiness
I'm sorry I can't be around to see it.

Freundschaft

Outside my door, the world seems to hum along.
Like the instruments of an orchestra
slotting in place for the grandest symphony.
The beat of hooves sticking to the path.
An unsettled whine permeates the air.
The seas of people sing along.

Outside I see -
A group of people sitting pressed together.
Their voices overlapped with laughter.
Reaching a deafening cacophony.
A piercing lullaby,
That I do not know the words to.

I cover my eardrums with my palms.
Tell me, is it so loud for you?

Every day I am deafened by the sound.
My ears are ringing.
Somewhere, there is a record player skipping.
The people laughing outside always leave,
eventually.
Is it really this hard for everyone?

The world keeps humming below.
Surely I can't stay still like a stuck record.
Caught in a groove.
Caught in a groove.
Caught in a groove.
I can't jump back and forth until I die.

I've been trying to learn the symphony.
Learn the lyrics to the song.
Learn how to get along better.
But when I open my mouth
Nothing comes out
I'll just try to forget it.

Things

There are an infinite amount of things that exist:
Washing Machines
Button Up Blouses
Hair Ties
Jet Planes
Blisteringly Warm Days
Mosquitos
Ceramic Bowls
and more.

There are also an infinite amount of things that
barely exist:
the left sock that went missing
half-eaten meals
5 am on a Wednesday morning
empty hallways
luggage that belongs to no one
pictures of empty rooms
and days that you don't feel anything at all

The Sea

You can abandon your problems at sea.
Get yourself a little rowboat.
Row out past the dock.

Far away until you can't see the city lights.
Make sure no one is around.
Dump your problems into the dark ocean water.

There is a small, but ever-present likelihood-
it will come back to haunt you as a Sea Ghost.
But that chance is very small.

I'm Over it Now

How do you know when you're over something?

Is it when you don't feel a desperate urge to talk
about it when you're six wines deep?

When you can stop writing shitty poetry about
it?

Or when you can tell jokes about it?

It's not like the scab is healing,
but it is not gushing blood anymore.

People

People notice
Sitting on a bus
Hands folded in prayer
Eyes squeezed shut
You got a new haircut
-it's nice.

People notice
and I don't know what's worse
The shame that everybody knows
Or betrayal that nobody cares

Sometimes

Sometimes I miss the girl who wanted more.

I think about her dreams
I miss her ideas and imagination.
Sometimes I remember the dazzling highs and
crushing lows.
It's not like that anymore.

Sometimes I tuck her into bed
and whisper goodnight.
Promise her someday- maybe.
Kiss her on the forehead,
but she had to go
So that I can stay.

I could never stand the noise of a big city.
My first failure sent me to the hospital.
I never had the drive to change.

I had to settle to be not great or bad,
but okay.

I don't crave the highs.
I don't miss the lows.
I sit in quiet mediocrity
and thank god that I can stand it.

The Man

He lies down in the dirt
"I'll rest here a little while"

The world goes on
There are mornings and nights
The train leaves the station
and comes back again.
He nestles his head into the dirt a little.

People have children
Those children have babies of their own
Meals are eaten and clothes are cleaned
Taxes are … whatever is done to taxes,
I suppose.
The vines start to wrap around his feet.

He doesn't move
Moss grows around his face
Leaves poke from his knees
Tree trunks pierce their roots into his lungs
He will get up soon.
He just needs to rest a little while.

Closing Time

I wrote you a thousand letters

all of them said

'stay'

even though I was the one leaving.

This is not a poem about you.

I'm Tired

Maybe one day someone will ask you,
why you pound clenched fists
against your chest and snarl with bared teeth and
roar at nothing
but how can you explain there is a wild beast
inside your skull?
A snarling wounded creature
and the measures you must go to each day
to get out of bed when it lurks in every doorway.
Nipping at your heels until they are bleeding.
Exhausted, always fighting a wild thing.

I have more control over the tides
Than I do over my mind.

But how can I explain?
The way I pound my chest too hard
until I break my sternum open
and pull out my bloody pumping heart and my
twisted stomach
and my blackened lungs.
Slowly unpack all the rest and clean them like
newborns
and I apologise every day for the things I've
done to them.

The ways I've sacrificed them for my peace of
mind.
I thank them and my heart beats on.
My body always fought on when I wanted to
give up.

Lessons

Your mother warned you not to touch broken
people

that you would cut yourself on their jagged
edges.

I come from rows of broken houses, broken tiny
hovels.

The first words I learnt were;

"I'm sorry."

Why Would I Tell You?

Something is wrong you say
You sense it
You ask me are you okay
I left the dirty dishes in the sink again

Everyone nods and understands
The empty seat at dinner
But they're resentful
The dishwasher is overflowing

You'll feel better if you come see me
I've been missing a lot of work
How will you get better
Rotting in bed surrounded by dirty dishes

Why would I tell you
We've had this conversation before
Are you okay?
No. I'm going to drown myself in the sink.